NATURAL WORLD

MOOSE

HABITATS • LIFE CYCLES • FOOD CHAINS • THREATS

Michael Leach

HODDER
Wayland

an imprint of Hodder
Children's Books

NATURAL WORLD

Black Rhino • Cheetah • Chimpanzee • Crocodile • Dolphin • Elephant
Giant Panda • Giraffe • Golden Eagle • Gorilla • Great White Shark
Grizzly Bear • Hippopotamus • Kangaroo • Killer Whale • Koala • Leopard
Lion • Moose • Orangutan • Penguin • Polar Bear • Seal • Tiger • Wolf • Zebra

Produced for Hodder Wayland by
Monkey Puzzle Media Ltd
Gissing's Farm, Fressingfield
Suffolk IP21 5SH, UK

Cover: An adult moose in North America.
Title page: A bull moose in Denali National Park, Alaska.
Contents page: Moose have large hooked noses that are very different to those of other deer.
Index page: Moose rarely move very far from water.

Published in Great Britain in 2003 by Hodder Wayland,
an imprint of Hodder Children's Books
Text copyright © 2003 Hodder Wayland
Volume copyright © 2003 Hodder Wayland

Editor: Angela Wilkes
Series editor: Victoria Brooker
Designer: Sarah Crouch

British Library Cataloguing in Publication Data
Leach, Michael, 1954-
  Moose. - (Natural World)
  Moose - Juvenile literature
  I.Title
  599.6'57

ISBN 0 7502 4384 8

Printed and bound by G. Canale & C.S.p.A., Turin, Italy

Hodder Children's Books
A division of Hodder Headline Limited
338 Euston Road, London NW1 3BH

Picture acknowledgements
FLPA 3 Helen Rhode, 7 Mark Newman, 9 David
Hosking, 10 Mark Newman, 14 Minden Pictures, 17
W Wisniewski, 19 Minden Pictures, 22 W Wisniewski,
25 Steve McCutcheon, 28 Mark Newman, 36 Helen
Rhode, 39 Minden Pictures, 44 top Mark Newman, 45
top Steve McCutcheon, 45 bottom W Wisniewski;
Nature Picture Library 8 David Kjaer, 12 Andrew
Harrington, 13 Mary Ann McDonald, 16 Bengt
Lundberg, 18 Naturbild, 21 Doug Wechsle, 24 Ingo
Arndt, 30 Jose Schell, 44 middle Andrew Harrington,
44 bottom Bengt Lundberg, 45 middle Doug Wechsle;
NHPA 1 Stephen Krasemann, 15 John Shaw, 23
Stephen Krasemann, 26 T Kitchin and V Hurst, 27
John Shaw, 31 John Shaw, 34 Paal Hermansen, 35
Stephen Krasemann, 38 Paal Hermansen, 42 Dr
Eckart Pott, 43 Roger Tidman, 48 Stephen
Krasemann; *OSF* 11 Bob Bennett, 20 Wendy Shattil
and Bob Rozinski, 29 Berndt Fisher, 32 Frank Huber,
37 Philippe Henry, 40 Tom Ulrich, 41 Edward
Robinson; *Science Photo Library* front cover C K
Lorenz, 6 Tony Comacho. Artwork by Michael Posen.

Contents

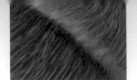

Meet the Moose

The moose is the largest member of the deer family. It has long legs, a huge hooked nose and a big flap of skin beneath its neck. Moose live in northern woodlands close to rivers or lakes. They are solitary animals and spend most of the year living alone. The only time they gather together is during the mating season.

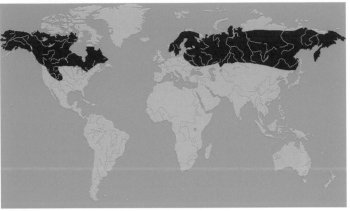

▲ The red shading on this map shows where moose live.

MOOSE FACTS

In Europe, moose are known as elk.

•

The word moose comes from an Algonquin Indian word for 'twig-eater'.

•

The scientific name for moose is *Alces alces*, from the Greek word *alke*, meaning 'strength'.

•

A male moose can weigh 600 kilograms, stand 2.25 metres high at the shoulder and measure up to 2.9 metres from nose to tail. Females are slightly smaller and weigh up to 500 kilograms. Only males have antlers.

Antlers
Male moose have large, flattened antlers that can spread up to 1.5 metres wide.

Eyes
Moose are very short-sighted. They can spot things moving but cannot see far into the distance. Their eyes are adapted to see underwater.

Ears
A moose has excellent hearing. Its ears can swivel in different directions to pinpoint any sound of approaching danger.

Shoulders
Moose have unmistakable humped shoulders. No other deer has this shape.

Fur
Thick dark fur keeps the moose warm in winter and acts as perfect camouflage amongst the dark shadow of a forest.

Tail
A moose has a short tail about 8 centimetres long.

Nose
Moose have a superb sense of smell. Their nostrils close completely when they go underwater to feed. This stops water from flooding into their lungs.

Legs
Long legs enable the moose to reach leaves growing high in the trees. They are also useful when walking in deep water. Each hind leg has a small claw that sticks out and helps stop the moose sinking into soft mud.

Bell
This is a distinctive flap of skin that hangs from a moose's neck. It can be 50 centimetres long and does not appear to have any particular purpose.

Hooves
The moose's large hooves splay out sideways when it walks. This spreads the moose's huge weight and makes it easier to walk over boggy ground.

▲ An adult moose

Moose relatives

All deer are members of a group known as the ungulates. This covers more than 200 species of mammal that have hooves instead of claws or toes. Other members of the group are giraffes, horses, pigs and camels. Ungulates first appeared on Earth about 54 million years ago. They are now one of the most numerous and widespread animal groups in the world. Many ungulates have horns. These are bony growths on the head that slowly grow bigger and remain throughout the animal's life. Deer have antlers that grow and drop off once every year.

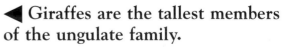
◀ Giraffes are the tallest members of the ungulate family.

MOOSE NAMES

A male moose is known as a bull and a female is called a cow. A moose's antlers are known as a 'rack'. The spikes are called tines. A mature male moose may have 30 tines on its rack. No two antler racks are exactly the same. They are all different shapes and sizes.

Today there are 34 living members of the deer family, ranging in size from the huge moose down to the tiny pudu, which lives in South America and weighs just eight kilograms. Deer are found throughout North and South America, Europe and Asia. Some species have been imported to parts of the world where they are not naturally found. During the nineteenth century, European settlers released fallow deer in South America and red deer in New Zealand. Both types of deer thrived and bred in their new homes.

▲ The southern pudu, from South America, is the smallest deer in the world. It is only 38 centimetres high and lives in very dense forests.

7

▲ Moose are often found in birch forests.

Habitat

Moose live in the great northern forests of the USA, Canada, Scandinavia and Russia. They were once found over a much larger area but hunting and the widespread destruction of forests wiped them out in many places. Moose prefer mixed forests that contain many different species of trees, such as spruce and willow. They usually stay away from large coniferous woodlands where there is little for them to eat. They particularly like areas of forest that have recently burned down. There they feed on the tender young saplings that spring up where the old trees used to grow.

Although these huge moose are very powerful and quite capable of killing a human, they are usually shy and carefully avoid people. Moose are large, heavy animals but they can walk through a forest without making a sound and often pass close to humans without being noticed. They are only really dangerous during the breeding season or when taken by surprise.

▼ This bull clearly shows the humped shoulders that are only found in moose.

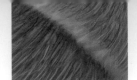

A Moose is Born

▶ This female moose has given birth amongst deep undergrowth, to keep her newborn calf safely hidden from passing enemies.

BABY MOOSE

A young moose is known as a calf. It weighs about 16 kilograms at birth. Unlike most deer, a moose calf has no spots. Young female moose normally have one calf, but as they get older they often give birth to twins. Sometimes triplets are born, but the youngest triplet usually dies.

A female moose gives birth to her calf in a quiet spot in the forest or amongst long grass. The newborn calf is covered with hair and its eyes are already open. The mother carefully licks her calf all over. This cleans it and helps both mother and calf to learn each other's scent. When the calf first struggles to its feet, it is weak and falls over. But by the time it is four hours old it can stand and walk, although it is still very wobbly.

BIRTH SEASON

Most moose calves are born in May and June. About half of them die before they reach the age of three months. The calves are reddish-brown when born, but this colour becomes darker as they grow older. Calves start suckling about 30 minutes after birth. They eat their first solid food at just four or five days old but they continue to suckle until they are about six months old.

▼ Young moose calves stay very close to their mother until they can run fast enough to escape from predators.

The young calf is not strong enough to keep up with its mother while she searches for food. For the first few days of its life, it remains safely hidden in deep undergrowth, silent and motionless. Its mother returns during the day, so the calf can feed on her milk. Calves are very vulnerable at this time. Many are killed by bears, which track them down by following their scent.

When the calf is about 5 days old, it joins its mother on her feeding trips. It also starts to take its first solid food. It carefully watches its mother and simply eats the same food as her.

Growing up

The moose calf grows and learns quickly. By the age of three weeks it can already swim. This means it can start eating the water plants that will make up much of its diet in the future. The calf can walk a long way but cannot move as quickly as its mother, so she has to keep a watchful eye open for predators. She is careful to keep away from any other big animals, even other moose. If danger threatens, the mother makes a bleating sound, like a sheep. The calf immediately returns to her and hides underneath her.

▼ Moose calves learn about the world by copying their mothers.

12

DANGEROUS MOOSE

Female moose will attack humans to defend their calves. Always keep well away from a mother with a calf. Even if a female moose seems to be alone, do not approach because there may be a calf hidden in the trees and you could accidentally walk between the mother and her calf. The mother would think you were threatening her calf, and she would immediately attack.

Female moose are very protective and will attack any animal that comes close to their calves. Bears are the biggest threat to a calf until it is about two weeks old but a young moose is soon fast enough to outrun a grizzly. Then wolves become the greatest danger. When facing a whole pack, a female moose can drive a few wolves away, but in the meantime others may approach from behind to attack her calf.

▲ Bears can pick up the scent of a calf up to one kilometre away. Grizzly bears often eat moose calves just a few hours after they are born.

▲ Moose often give birth to twins. But predators may take one of the calves because their mother cannot defend both youngsters at the same time.

Becoming independent

By the age of five months, the moose calf weighs 150 kilograms. It stops suckling when it is about six months old. The young moose needs to put on plenty of weight if it is going to survive the long, cold winter ahead, when good food will be hard to find. During the next six months the calf will grow at the rate of two kilograms every day. Weak calves often die of starvation during their first winter.

Young moose stay with their mother until they are about a year old. By then, the mother is ready to give birth again and the calf is big enough to look after itself. As the time approaches to give birth, the mother looks for a quiet hiding place. The calf has followed its mother around for its whole life and does not want to leave her. She charges at it to chase it away. Most calves return to their mother a few minutes later. A female moose often attacks her calf several times before it gives up and leaves for good.

▼ A female moose and her calf wading into shallow water to feed.

Learning to Survive

The young moose starts to look after itself in early summer when there is plenty of food around. It has no difficulty finding a suitable patch of forest because moose are not territorial animals. They only drive off rivals during the breeding season. Each moose wanders freely through the forest in search of good feeding areas.

▲ This young European elk is losing its thick winter coat. Beneath is much shorter, cooler summer fur.

FEEDING TECHNIQUES

Moose eat the leaves growing on trees. This is known as browsing. They also eat grass and other plants growing on the ground. This type of feeding is called grazing.

▼ Large antlers can cause problems when a bull moose is trying to walk through very thick forests.

The size of a moose feeding range depends upon the habitat. In areas where food is scarce there may be just one adult to a square kilometre of forest. But where food is plentiful there may be up to eight moose to every square kilometre. The big males usually take the first pick of the best food, however, and smaller moose keep away.

Moose live alone, but there are often other moose nearby. At first the young moose is careful to avoid meeting other moose, as bulls sometimes attack youngsters for no reason. Adult moose are at their heaviest and strongest around the age of six years.

Keeping cool

In the summer, the moose is most active around dusk and dawn. It can quickly overheat in hot weather, so it needs to shelter from the direct sunlight. It sometimes just wanders into the forest and lies down in the shade of trees. But it often stands in deep water, where it feeds and can keep cool. Moose are surprisingly well camouflaged in rivers and lakes, standing with just their heads above the surface of the water. Eventually they have to come ashore to rest and sleep.

▼ Moose often like to rest beneath trees during the hottest time of the day.

WATER DEER

Moose are extremely well adapted to water. They have been known to swim 20 kilometres without resting and often dive up to 5.5 metres down into lakes to reach underwater plants.

▲ Moose sometimes stand still in lakes and rivers, without feeding. The water all around them keeps them safe from most predators.

Out of the water, the moose is followed by thousands of flies. Some fly species lay their eggs in moose's noses or under their skin. To avoid the flies, the moose digs shallow hollows called scrapes in the ground with its front feet. These are about 1.25 metres square and 10 centimetres deep. Rain soon fills the scrapes and forms mud. The moose wallows in the mud, rolling over again and again to cover its entire body. The mud soon dries, forming a hard protective coat that helps keep off the flies.

▲ When autumn comes, moose spend most of their time eating. Soon the leaves will fall from the trees and the moose must be prepared for several months of hunger.

Preparing for winter

In the autumn, the moose eats huge amounts of food. This is stored as a layer of fat just beneath the skin and will help it to survive the winter. As the temperatures drop, the forest slowly changes and life becomes far more difficult for moose. They have to spend all day searching for enough food to stay alive. If the weather becomes too bad or if all the food disappears, moose leave their normal feeding grounds to look for somewhere better. They have been known to migrate more than 300 kilometres in just three months.

By the end of winter, the snow can be a metre thick and covered with a layer of ice. Although this deep snow hides plants growing on the ground, it is hard enough to walk on and means that the moose can now browse from high branches that would be out of reach in summer. In winter, the moose's coat becomes much thicker and turns slightly greyer. This warm coat will moult when spring comes again.

▼ A thick, warm coat protects the moose against temperatures that may drop as low as –35° centigrade.

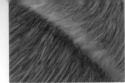

Family Life

▲ Fights between bulls often only last for a few minutes. The weaker bull usually walks away before he is injured.

Moose do not live in herds, although they sometimes gather together in good feeding areas. The males and females ignore each other for most of the year and only come into contact during the breeding season. This is known as the rut and takes place in September and October.

GIANT MOOSE

The largest moose on record was discovered in Alaska in 1897. It measured 2.34 metres at the shoulder, weighed 816 kilograms and had antlers measuring 1.99 metres across.

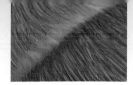

Before mating, a bull moose has to establish a territory of his own in order to attract females. The moose shows off its strength by thrashing its antlers against trees and leaves. It also urinates in its scrapes, then rolls around in the mud to absorb the scent into its coat. This smell is carried on the wind and warns rivals to keep away. If another bull tries to invade his territory, the moose roars, lowers his antlers and charges his rival. This is usually enough to make the invader run off.

When two bulls are evenly matched, they push each other in a contest of strength. They use their antlers as weapons but serious battles are rare, as one bull usually backs down before being injured. Very occasionally two bulls' sets of antlers become interlocked. Both bulls will die unless they can get free.

► Antlers are very heavy so bull moose need large, powerful neck muscles to hold up their heads.

23

▼ During the rutting season, bull moose use their excellent sense of smell to find females. A female's scent can be carried several kilometres by the wind.

Finding a mate

Eventually the largest, strongest bulls win control of their territories and make a series of low, loud roars to let other moose know. These calls warn off rivals and attract the attention of nearby females, who call back in return. The bull's call is loud and short. A female makes a much longer sound. When a female calls, the bull follows the sound. He will only approach her if she is inside his territory. If he enters another bull's territory he will be attacked.

▲ Bull moose keep very close to females during the breeding season. They usually stay within a few metres of each other.

Once the bull has found a female, he stays with her for about a week and they mate many times. The bull is very protective and immediately charges if a moose or any other animal comes anywhere near. After mating, the bull leaves and goes in search of another female. He will mate with any female that comes into his territory. This can be as many as ten females in one season. At the end of the mating season the bull plays no part at all in raising the calves.

▲ Two bull moose display at each other, trying to decide which is the strongest.

The breeding season

During the rutting season most bulls stop eating altogether for up to four weeks. They spend many hours patrolling their territory, looking for rivals and females. Mating, fighting and lack of food make bulls lose weight. By the end of the rutting season some bulls have lost up to 20 per cent of their body weight and they become slow and clumsy. They may be driven away from their territory by bulls that have not yet mated and are still strong. Hunger and exhaustion also makes bulls weak and vulnerable to attack by predators. Tired bulls cannot defend themselves against efficient enemies, such as wolves. As a result, more bulls are killed just after the breeding season than at any other time of the year.

The female moose finish the breeding season in much better condition and nearly all of them will be pregnant. The calves are born eight months after mating. Moose cows usually have calves every year until they die.

▼ Antlers rarely fall off at the same time. Once one is lost, the moose's head is unbalanced and is pulled down to one side until the other antler drops.

ANGRY BULLS

During the breeding season bull moose become very aggressive and unpredictable. They may attack anything that comes close to them, including other animals, cars, humans and even trains.

Back to normal

Once the rutting season is over, bull moose stop being so aggressive, leave their territories and spend all their time eating. In December and January, their antlers snap at the base and drop off. Antlers are a good source of minerals such as calcium. Once on the ground, they are chewed by small animals, such as mice and voles. Even deer have been known to nibble them. After a few weeks the antlers are covered with teeth marks of various sizes. Within three months they have been completely eaten.

▲ Growing antlers need lots of nourishment. When they drop off, bull moose do not grow new ones until the spring. In winter moose need their food to stay alive, instead of using it to produce antlers.

MOOSE ANTLERS

Moose have the largest antlers in the world. A mature male can have a pair measuring 1.5 metres across. They grow to this size in just five months, appearing in April and reaching full size in August. They are one of the fastest growing structures in the animal world.

A bull's new antlers start to show in March. At first they look like small furry lumps on top of the moose's head but they grow incredibly quickly. A full set of antlers will grow in six months and will be ready for the next breeding season. A bull moose's antlers are at their biggest when the animal is about six years old. From then on, the antlers do not grow as large and they start to look deformed.

▶ Moose nostrils face downward to help prevent water entering their noses while they feed in lakes.

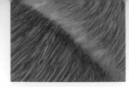

Finding Food

A moose is a herbivore, which means that it only eats plants. It feeds on a wide variety of vegetation including grass, pondweed, water lilies and horsetails. It spends a lot of time feeding underwater, feasting on the rich variety of plants that grow beneath the surface. Moose spend most of the summer feeding in rivers and lakes and only come out of the water to sleep.

▼ In summer, water provides food, protection from biting flies and helps keep a moose cool.

▲ A moose's lips are delicate and sensitive. It uses them for picking the best leaves from a tree.

A GIANT APPETITE

The average moose eats around 20 kilograms of food every day. This rises to a huge 59 kilograms in the autumn, when the moose is building up fat ready for the long, cold winter ahead.

Moose also browse on the leaves of trees such as birch, willow and aspen. They are particularly fond of the fresh young leaves that grow at the ends of branches. A moose often grabs a branch and pulls hard. It then strips off the leaves with its lips and tongue, leaving the wood attached to the tree. A moose has a unique way of reaching the top leaves of saplings. It pushes its chest against the slender tree trunk and slowly walks forwards. The sapling bends over, making it easy for the moose to reach the leaves growing at the top.

Chewing the cud

Leaves and other parts of plants are tough and difficult to digest. Like all deer, a moose has a special way of handling this kind of food. It eats very quickly, nipping off leaves and twigs, then swallowing them immediately without chewing. A human stomach is made up of just one chamber but a moose's stomach is divided into four chambers. When the moose swallows food, it passes into the first chamber and is simply stored. After eating for a few hours, the chamber is full. The moose then finds a safe resting-place and coughs the food it has eaten back up into its mouth in small chunks, so it can chew it.

▼ This bull moose is chewing the cud after feeding for several hours.

MOOSE FOOD CHAIN

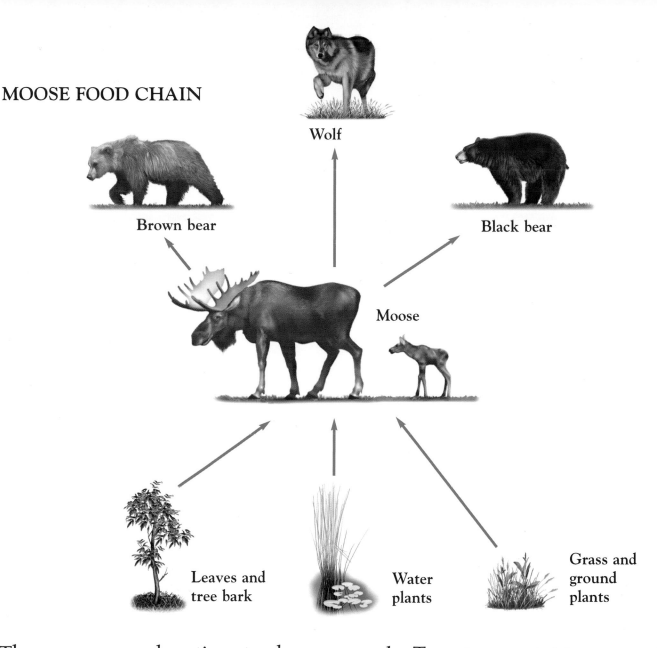

The moose now has time to chew properly. Twenty-four large teeth called premolars and molars at the back of its mouth grind the food it has eaten, to make it soft and moist. The food is then swallowed again and passes into the moose's second stomach chamber and on through the rest of its digestive system. This way of eating is known as chewing the cud. Many other animals, such as cows, eat in the same way. Moose often spend more time chewing the cud than they do collecting food.

▲ Moose eat only plants, but they are preyed upon by large predators such as bears and wolves.

The search for food

Moose do not like mature thick forests, because
most of the food is too high for them to reach.
They prefer open woodlands with space between
the trees where plants grow on the ground. Bulls
have great trouble feeding in dense forest,
because their huge antlers get caught in branches
and twigs. Females sometimes push through
thick undergrowth but males will usually walk
around it, even if it means a long detour.

▲ Moose sometimes
eat agricultural crops,
such as these oats.

Moose occasionally leave the forest to raid farmland and eat agricultural crops. Farmers shoot any moose that make a habit of feeding in their fields. Moose regularly enter the city of Anchorage in Alaska to feed on garden plants. They have now become a regular sight walking through town and they often cause traffic jams by simply standing in the middle of roads and refusing to move. Moose and humans have learned to ignore each other, but there are problems when dogs appear. Moose do not like dogs and they usually attack them immediately.

MOOSE HEDGE

In some forests, moose create feeding lines by eating all the tree branches up to about 2 metres high. The lower branches of the trees form a flat ceiling and look as if gardeners have pruned them into shape.

▼ Moose will travel long distances in search of new feeding areas.

Surviving the winter

Animals need more food in winter as they require extra energy to keep warm when temperatures are low. Unfortunately the water plants that moose eat during the summer soon disappear when winter begins. Some lakes and rivers are covered with ice nearly a metre thick, which may not melt until April. In Alaska and northern Europe and Asia, winter can last for more than six months.

▲ Grass and other ground plants are often covered with very deep snow during the winter. Moose sometimes scrape away the snow with their feet to reach the food beneath.

Moose need to change their food to survive and they will eat anything available. In summer, moose are careful eaters and only take leaves from trees, but in winter they will eat entire branches. When the leaves have all gone, moose use their sharp lower incisors to scrape the bark off trees so that they can eat the rich, nutritious layer beneath, called cambium. By the end of winter, moose may have lost 20 per cent of their bodyweight. When the weather is particularly bad or if winter lasts longer than normal, some animals cannot find enough food and starve to death before spring returns.

▼ The bark of this tree has been stripped off and eaten by moose. The tree may die if it has lost too much bark.

MOOSE TEETH

Moose have no incisor teeth in their top jaw. When they eat, their lower incisors bite against the tough leathery gums above. This is strong enough to snap even the strongest branches.

37

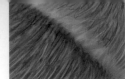

Threats

Moose calves are killed by bears, wolves, mountain lions and lynx, but fully-grown moose are strong enough to defend themselves against most predators. Although grizzly bears occasionally kill adult moose, they usually only manage to catch animals that are old or ill. Wolves are the moose's only major enemy. In Alaska a single wolf pack kills one moose every week on average.

MOOSE POPULATION

Moose are not an endangered species. Their numbers are slowly growing in many areas. A moose can live up to the age of 20.

▼ Moose are big and heavy but they can run surprisingly fast.

Moose rarely run away when they are threatened. They turn to face the danger and defend themselves by lashing out with their powerful front legs. A single kick from a moose's huge hoof can kill a fully-grown wolf. Bulls also attack by lowering their heads and charging. Their huge antlers can severely wound a wolf or bear. Wolves are very careful when hunting moose. The wolf pack splits up and surrounds the moose. The moose can protect itself from the wolves in front of it, but it cannot see those behind. Each wolf darts in and tries to grab one of the moose's legs. As soon as one wolf has a good hold on the moose, the rest of the pack moves in for the kill.

▲ A charging bull moose is one of the most dangerous animals in the northern forests.

Struggle for survival

A moose that is being chased by wolves often plunges into a river or lake. Moose have much longer legs than wolves, so they can stand in deep water while their enemies are forced to swim. This extra height makes it easier for the moose to kick. It can also dive underwater if the wolves come too close. Even a hungry pack of wolves will give up after a few minutes, so moose survive most encounters in the water.

▲ Moose are an important prey species for wolves.

SPEEDY MOOSE

Moose can run at speeds of up to 56 kilometres per hour and swim at nearly 10 kilometres per hour.

Moose are at their most vulnerable in winter. Snow often covers the ground for a long time in the forests. Heavy snow makes walking slow and running almost impossible. A moose caught in a drift of soft snow cannot turn quickly when attacked by enemies. Deep snow also makes it difficult for moose to use their long legs for kicking.

Moose are a very important part of the food chain. One adult moose provides food for a whole wolf pack for several days and scavengers, such as ravens, wolverines and even lynx, eat any scraps left behind.

▼ By the end of winter, moose are usually thin, weak and very hungry.

Moose and humans

In both Europe and North America, moose are killed by licensed hunters armed with rifles. In Alaska alone, about 7,000 moose are shot every year. Many more are killed illegally by poachers for their meat. Moose are common in some National Parks in Canada and the United States. Tourists try to feed them but this is dangerous because moose often attack when the food runs out. Moose can run much faster than humans, who can only escape by climbing a tree or hiding behind something big, such as a car. However, angry moose have been known to wait for several hours before they give up and leave.

▼ Moose in popular tourist areas often lose their fear of humans and learn to beg for food.

DOMESTICATED ELK

In Russia, during the twentieth century, there were several attempts to keep elk for the production of meat and milk. They were also trained to pull wagons, particularly in winter when other animals could not handle the snowy conditions. But the elk were too dangerous and unpredictable and the idea was quickly dropped.

▲ Drivers are warned to keep a careful look out for moose on roads throughout forests in Canada and Scandinavia.

EXTINCT MOOSE

Moose were once much more common and widespread than they are today. During the Middle Ages, elk lived in the huge forests that covered western and central Europe. But they were hunted to extinction, mainly for their meat.

Moose are a major problem on the roads in some areas of Canada. They often walk along the highway looking for new feeding areas. When an animal the size of a moose is hit by a vehicle travelling at 80 kilometres per hour, both can be very badly damaged. Drivers are sometimes killed in moose collisions and these accidents cause hundreds of moose deaths every year.

Moose Life Cycle

 **1** A moose calf is covered in hair and has its eyes open when it is born. It can walk within two hours of birth.

 **2** By the time the calf is five days old, it is strong enough to walk and follow its mother.

 **3** Young moose leave their mother at the age of 12 months and find their own feeding range.

 Moose can mate at the age of one year but they rarely have young.

 A female moose has her first calf when she is two years of age.

 At the age of five, male moose are big enough to fight rivals and win the right to mate.

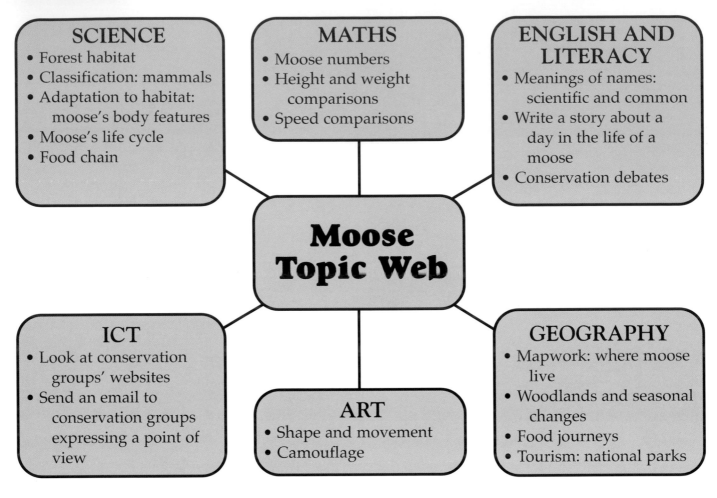

SCIENCE
- Forest habitat
- Classification: mammals
- Adaptation to habitat: moose's body features
- Moose's life cycle
- Food chain

MATHS
- Moose numbers
- Height and weight comparisons
- Speed comparisons

ENGLISH AND LITERACY
- Meanings of names: scientific and common
- Write a story about a day in the life of a moose
- Conservation debates

Moose Topic Web

ICT
- Look at conservation groups' websites
- Send an email to conservation groups expressing a point of view

ART
- Shape and movement
- Camouflage

GEOGRAPHY
- Mapwork: where moose live
- Woodlands and seasonal changes
- Food journeys
- Tourism: national parks

Extension Activities

English
- Debate whether moose should be kept in zoos.
- Find and list collective names for groups of animals, or terms for their young, eg. calf, chick, cub.

Geography
- Trace a world map from an atlas. Show the location of all the places mentioned in this book.
- Draw a map showing where moose live.

Maths
- Use the moose's face and antlers as a model to develop work on symmetry.

Art
- Make a forest frieze, showing moose and the other animals that live there.

Science
- Make a display showing the ways in which moose are adapted to live in their habitat.

Glossary

Bell A large flap of skin hanging beneath a moose's chin.

Browsing Eating leaves directly from the trees.

Camouflage The colour or pattern on an animal that helps it to blend in with the surroundings.

Endangered A species that is in danger of completely dying out.

Extinct Died out completely; no longer alive anywhere.

Grazing Eating plants, mainly grass, which grow low down on the ground.

Habitat The area where an animal lives.

Herbivore An animal that only eats plants.

Incisor Sharp cutting tooth at the front of the mouth.

Migrate To make a long journey, usually in search of better conditions, such as more food.

Poacher People who kill wild animals illegally.

Predator An animal that kills and eats other animals.

Prey An animal that is killed and eaten by other animals.

Rut The time of year when moose mate.

Suckle A young animal drinking milk from its mother's teats.

Territory The area that is defended and patrolled by an animal.

Ungulates Animals with hooves.

Wallow Lie and roll in water or mud.

Further Information

Organizations to Contact

The British Deer Society
Fordingbridge
Hampshire SP6 1EF
Tel: 01425 655434
Website: www.bds.org.uk

The North American Moose
Foundation, PO Box 30,
610 W. Custer, Suite D,
Mackay Idaho 83251, USA
Tel: 001 208 588 2939
Website:
www.moosefoundation.org

Books to Read

North American Moose by Lesley A Dutemple (Carolrhoda Books Inc, 2000)
Moose (Naturebooks) by Jenny Markert (Child's World Inc, 1999)
Moose by Daniel Wood (Whitecap Books, 1999)
Moose: Gentle Giants of the Northern Forest by Bill Silliker (Firefly Books Ltd, 1998)

Moose (World Life Library) by Art Rodgers (Voyageur Press, 2001)
Moose (Our Wild World Series) by Anthony Fredericks & John F McGee (Northword Press, 2000)
The Moose (Wildlife of North America) by Annie Hemstock (Capstone High-Interest Books, 1999)

Index

Page numbers in **bold** refer to photographs or illustrations.